A BRIEF HISTORY OF THE UKULELE

Most ukulele historians agree that the birth of the ukulele began in 1879, when Portuguese agricultural workers arrived in Honolulu aboard the English ship *Ravenscrag*. Many of these workers—like Augusto Dias, Manuel Nunes, Joao Fernandes, Joao Luiz Correa, and Jose do Espirito Santo—brought with them a remarkable ability to play the machete (a small guitar-like instrument with four cat-gut strings, the precursor to the uke). In turn, these workers also shared an intense passion for working with wood, and thus began a rich tradition of ukulele craftsmanship on the islands.

The year 1915 brought with it the Pan-Pacific International Exposition held in San Francisco. Here, the Hawaiian contingent and their beloved ukulele helped to spark its popular appeal amongst players and consumers alike. What followed were Hawaiian-themed songs and musicians, a sheet-music industry that regularly printed ukulele chord symbols on its music, uke-strumming Vaudeville entertainers, and mainland manufacturing companies like Martin, Gibson, Harmony, Lyon & Healy, and Epiphone all working overtime to meet the demand for quality ukes.

Some of the greatest players to emerge from this early era included Cliff Edwards (Ukulele Ike), Wendell Hall (The Red-Headed Uke Player), Johnny Marvin (Honey Duke), Roy Smeck, Frank Crumit, King Bennie Nawahi, Ukulele Bailey, and George Formby (in the UK).

While the depression years of the 1930s and the war years of the forties may have brought a temporary lapse of interest, uke hysteria began anew in the 1950s with the appearance of baritone uke player Arthur Godfrey, whose numerous television and radio appearances helped to put the ukulele back in the limelight. In the next decade, Tiny Tim's 1968 novelty cover of the Nick Lucas tune "Tiptoe Through the Tulips" made quite a splash, and it's safe to say it is still the best-known uke song amongst non-players in the U.S.

Today's ukulele revival is experiencing a groundswell of interest amongst both the young and old, while drawing from traditional and eclectic sources. There is a vitality to the current crop of professional players, all of whom treat the uke with a lot of historic respect while continuing to push the envelope in many new directions. We are just as likely to hear Canadian virtuoso James Hill play his incredible rendition of the "Super Mario Brothers" theme as we are to hear the young Hawaiian star Jake Shimabukuro play Paul Simon's "Mrs. Robinson," or for that matter, ukulele guru Jumpin' Jim Beloff croon the classic "Bye Bye Blackbird."

So ya see, once you learn the basics of picking and strumming, the sky is the limit... for the history is still being written!

Cliff Edwards: the Golden Voice of the 1920s and '30s.

Courtesy of David Garrick

George Formby: the Uke Star of the U.K.

From BBC Picture Archives/Redferns

Tiny Tim: broke into pop culture with his novelty cover of the Nick Lucas tune "Tip Toe Through the Tulips."

Photo by Dick Barnatt/Redferns

YOUR UKULELE

This book is designed for use with any type of soprano, concert, or tenor ukulele—whether they are wood-bodied, banjo-ukulele, or resonator-style ukuleles. You may use any of these models to study the music in this manual.

Wood-Bodied Ukulele

Headstock

Fretboard

Strings

Soundhole

Resonator Ukulele

Banjo-Ukulele

Body

Bridge

HAL LEONARD

UKULELE METHOD

BY LIL' REV

	PAGE
Introduction	2
A Brief History of the Ukulele	3
Your Ukulele	4
Playing Position	5
Tuning	6
Musical Symbols	7
Notes on the C String	8
Notes on the E String	9
Frére Jacques	10
Mary Had a Little Lamb	10
Go Tell Aunt Rhody	11
Ode to Joy	11
Notes on the A String	12
Twinkle, Twinkle Little Star	13
Oh! Susanna	15
The C Major Scale	16
High D and High E	17
Aura Lee	18
Wildwood Flower	19
Eighth Notes	20
Frére Jacques	20
Shortening Bread	21
Little Brown Jug	22
Playing Chords	23
C, F, and G7 Chords	23
Strumming Chords	24
Generic Blues	25
Strum It	26
The G Chord Family	27
G, C, D7, and Em Chords	27
Ooh-Wah Uke	27
Boil 'Em Cabbage Down	28
3/4 Time	29
Waltz	29
Waltz Strum	30

	PAGE
Amazing Grace	31
The F Chord Family	32
F, Bb, and C7 Chords	32
Hush Little Baby	32
Rolling	33
Juking the Uke	33
F-Sharp	34
Down in the Valley	34
B-Flat	35
Key Signatures	35
The F Major Scale	36
Clementine	36
Paw Paw Patch	37
Skip to My Lou	37
In the Moon's Pale Shimmer	38
She'll Be Coming 'Round the Mountain	38
The Single Roll Stroke	39
Shave and a Haircut	39
Playing Tremolo	40
Aura Lee	40
The Am Chord	41
Doo-Wop Uke	41
Rests	42
Goodnight Ladies	43
Merrily We Roll Along	43
The E Minor Chord Family	44
Em, Am, and B7 Chords	44
The Haunted Uke Blues	45
Hey, Ho, Nobody Home	45
More Chords	46
Dm and A7 Chords	46
Sinner Man	47
Scarborough Fair	47
Chord Chart	48

HAL•LEONARD® CORPORATION

7777 W. BLUEMOUND RD. P.O. BOX 13819 MILWAUKEE, WI 53213

ISBN 0-634-07986-7

Copyright © 2005 by HAL LEONARD CORPORATION
International Copyright Secured   All Rights Reserved

In Australia contact: **Hal Leonard Australia Pty. Ltd**.
4 Lentara Court, Cheltenham, Victoria, 3192 Australia
Email: ausadmin@halleonard.com

Visit Hal Leonard Online at **www.halleonard.com**

INTRODUCTION

Welcome to the Hal Leonard *Ukulele Method Book 1*. This method has been designed to help you accomplish your goal of becoming a proficient ukulele player. While there are many styles and techniques to learn from, this book will focus on individual note or melody playing.

Once you begin, you will find that the ukulele is a magical little instrument that always seems to attract a smile. It really has the power to make people happy. Whether it is the novelty of its size or its infectious rhythmic nature, you can expect that your endeavors to play the uke will result in a lot of toe-tapping, finger-snapping, hand-clapping, and plain old-fashioned singing along.

Over time, you will also find that the ukulele's potential extends far beyond the parameters of simple strumming to include fingerpicking, solo, lead and chord-melody playing, intricate strums, rolls, tremolo, slides, and a whole slew of rhythmic and novelty effects.

Practice may not always make perfect, but it sure helps to keep ya moving along. While it is important to work hard, please remember that music should first of all be fun! You don't have to practice for ten hours a day in order to improve. Rather, strive for more consistent practice over shorter periods of time. With diligence, soon you will master important techniques and concepts.

Good luck and happy strumming!

—Lil' Rev

Special Thanks to Jennifer Rupp, Will Branch, and Dennis Felber for technical assistance.

ABOUT THE AUTHOR

Lil' Rev is a Milwaukee, Wisconsin-based award-winning multi-instrumentalist, writer, and music historian. He tours the U.S. teaching and performing original and traditional folk, blues, ethnic, and old-time music.

To learn more about Lil' Rev's schedule, recordings, or programs, visit *www.lilrev.com*

PLAYING POSITION

There are many ways to hold your ukulele comfortably. Typically, you will be seated, but you may find it necessary to stand on occasion. See what works best for you.

The seated position allows you to rest the uke on your right leg. Or, apply a small amount of pressure with your right forearm to press the uke up against your right side rib cage.

The standing position takes a little more getting used to. You must apply a little more pressure with your right forearm to keep the uke in place.

Some folks like to use a strap to hold their uke in place.

THE RIGHT HAND

Once you are comfortable holding the uke, you will need to become familiar with the proper hand, thumb, and finger positions so that you will be able to pick and strum properly.

Hand

Hold your hand just slightly above the sound hole with your fingers extended over the fretboard.

Thumb

Place your thumb over the lower end of the fretboard for a gentle brush.

Finger

Slightly curl your right pointer finger inward and place it just above the tenth fret (you'll learn more about fret numbers soon).

TUNING

When you tune your ukulele, you will adjust the **pitch** (highness or lowness) of each individual string. When you tighten a string you will raise the pitch. When you loosen a string you will lower the pitch.

The strings on your uke are numbered 1 through 4, with string 4 being the one closest to your chest. This book uses the standard C tuning (the most common ukulele tuning), so your uke would be tuned as follows:

Pitch:	G	C	E	A
String:	4	3	2	1

TUNING WITH AN ELECTRONIC TUNER

An electronic tuner will "hear" whether or not your strings are in tune, allowing you to adjust them to the correct pitch. While I advocate learning how to tune by ear (being able to recognize and match the sound of a pitch without the help of a machine), an electronic tuner can be real handy when you are just starting out and have not yet developed the ability to recognize in-tune pitches. A tuner's accuracy and efficiency make it a useful tool.

TUNING BY EAR

Tune the G string (string 4) to a reliable source like a piano, tuning fork, or pitch pipe. Then tune the other strings to the following notes to create this musical phrase:

RELATIVE TUNING

Often, you may have to tune your instrument to itself when there is no other source available. To do this, follow these steps:

1. Assume the third string is tuned correctly to C.
2. Press down on the third string behind the fourth fret (E) and tune the second string until they sound alike.
3. Press down on the second string at the fifth fret (A) and tune the open first string to it.
4. Finally, press down on the second string above the third fret (G) and tune the fourth string to it.

When all of the strings are in tune, they will sound out the familiar musical phrase:

MUSICAL SYMBOLS

Music is written with notes on a **staff**. The staff has five lines and four spaces between the lines. Where a note is written on the staff determines its pitch (highness or lowness). At the beginning of the staff is a clef sign. Ukulele music is written in the treble clef.

STAFF

TREBLE CLEF

Each line and space of the staff has a letter name. The **lines** are (from bottom to top) E–G–B–D–F, which you can remember as "Every Good Boy Does Fine." The **spaces** are (from bottom to top) F–A–C–E, which spells "face."

LINES

E G B D F

SPACES

F A C E

The staff is divided into several parts by bar lines. The space between two bar lines is called a **measure** (also known as a "bar"). At the end of a piece of music a double bar is placed on the staff.

BAR LINES

MEASURE

BAR LINE   BAR LINE   DOUBLE BAR LINE (transition)   DOUBLE BAR LINE (end)

Each measure contains a group of **beats**. Beats are the steady pulse of music. You respond to the pulse or beat when you tap your foot.

The two numbers placed next to the clef sign are the **time signature**. The top number tells you how many beats are in one measure.

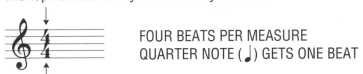

FOUR BEATS PER MEASURE
QUARTER NOTE (♩) GETS ONE BEAT

The bottom number of the time signature tells you what kind of note will receive one beat.

Notes indicate the length (number of counts) of a musical sound.

NOTE VALUES

WHOLE NOTE = 4 beats   HALF NOTE = 2 beats   QUARTER NOTE = 1 beat

When different kinds of notes are placed on different lines or spaces, you will know the pitch of the note and how long to play the sound.

NOTES ON THE C STRING

We begin learning notes on the C string, or third string, because in C tuning, the fourth (G) string is usually not fingered except when making chords. However, many players (like Hawaii's legendary Ohta San) tune the G string low so that it can be used for melody playing.

Play these whole notes using your thumb, and count "1–2–3–4."

Now try playing C and D using half notes. Count "1–2–3–4."

In **tablature** (or tab) notation, the horizontal lines represent strings. The numbers indicate which fret to play (0 = open). You'll always see the tab staff under the main staff.

Keep using your thumb, and count "1–2–3–4" while playing these quarter notes.

Let's mix it up a little more now!

NOTES ON THE E STRING

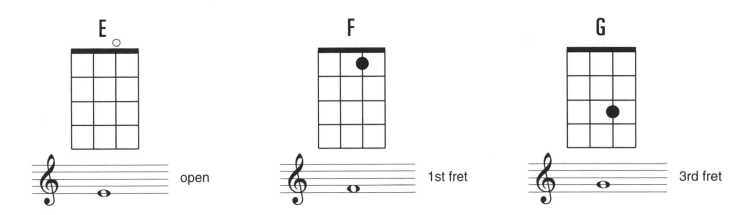

Count "1–2–3–4" as you did on the last exercise.

Each time you repeat these exercises, try picking up the speed without sacrificing accuracy.

Now let's mix it up again.

C AND E STRING REVIEW

FRÉRE JACQUES
(Are You Sleeping?)

Children's Melody

MARY HAD A LITTLE LAMB

This American folk melody, like "Skip to My Lou," "Old Dan Tucker," and so many other "play party" tunes, has become an enduring classic. Just for fun, I have added a schnazzy little ending.

Gray chord symbols are used throughout this book to indicate the chords that back up your melody—they can be played by an instructor or another uke player.

GO TELL AUNT RHODY

American Folk Song

This classical uke arrangement will help you get familiar with many of the notes you've just learned while switching back and forth between the C and E strings.

ODE TO JOY

Beethoven

NOTES ON THE A STRING

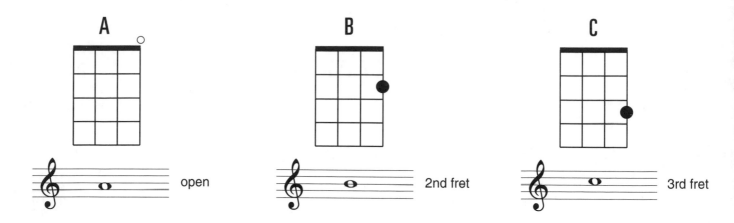

Count "1–2–3–4" as you did in the previous exercises.

Try saying each note aloud as you play it.

Now let's mix it up again.

Now let's play a basic melody everyone knows using the notes we've learned on the C, E, and A strings. Observe the quarter notes and half notes, and play with your thumb.

TWINKLE, TWINKLE LITTLE STAR

Children's Melody

Great melodies never stray too far from our hearts. Often they inspire parodies, like the classic "Twinkle, Twinkle Little Star," which we also know as "Bah Bah Black Sheep" and "The Alphabet Song."

Little known and often neglected is the great body of work recorded in the 1920s and thirties by old-time country, blues, and jug bands. Their use of the ukulele demonstrates not only its percussive role, but also the full gamut of uke styling—from intricate strums, rolls, and fingerpicking to tremolo and single-string lead work—all, of course, complimented by scat singing, whistling, yodeling, and other vocal embellishments of the period. Some of these important bands were the Hillbillies, Fiddlin' Powers Family, Jimmie Rodgers, Memphis Jug Band, and DaCosta Woltz's Southern Broadcasters.

PICKUP NOTES

Sometimes a melody will begin before the first beat of the first measure. These notes are called **pickup notes** and they appear in a partial measure called the **pickup measure**. Always remember to count the missing beats before playing your first pickup note. When a song begins with pickup notes, the last measure will be short the exact number of beats used as pickups.

The pickup measure in this exercise has only one quarter note. Count "1–2–3–" silently before playing the quarter note on beat 4. Notice that the last measure is short by one beat to balance out the one-beat pickup note.

The following pickup measure has two quarter notes. Count "1–2–" silently before playing beats 3 and 4.

DOTTED NOTES

When you see a **dotted note**, hold that note 50% longer than you would normally hold it. For example, a dotted half note (♩.) lasts as long as a half note plus a quarter note. A dot adds half the value of the note.

Watch for the dotted half notes on this one.

OH! SUSANNA

Stephen C. Foster

THE C MAJOR SCALE

PUTTIN' IT ALL TOGETHER

Begin by playing the scale in both directions, up and down. Use your thumb (or a felt-tip pick) and go slowly, gradually building up speed. While you are playing the scale, say the notes aloud as you pick them. When you can do this smoothly without breaking your rhythm, then you're ready to begin playing some more basic melodies.

Try playing up and down the C scale, picking twice per note. Your goal is to sound smooth and even.

HIGH D AND HIGH E

You already know the fingering for low D and E. Higher versions (or **octaves**) of these notes exist along the A string. Here they are:

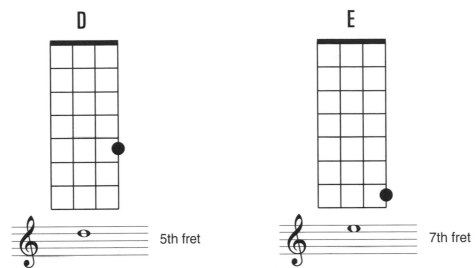

Try playing high D and high E using half notes. Count "1–2–3–4."

Remember, use your thumb and count while playing these quarter notes.

Let's mix it up a little more now!

This lovely folk melody was known as "Aura Lee" until 1956, when Elvis Presley's rendition made it popular as "Love Me Tender."

AURA LEE

Traditional

TIES

This symbol (⌣) is known as a **tie**. When you see two notes tied together (♩‿♩), even across measures, play them as a single note. In other words, you simply add the first note to the second and hold them out for the full duration of both notes.

In the twelfth measure of "Wildwood Flower," the number (3) over the first two notes means that you should play these notes with the third (or ring) finger of your left hand. Watch for ties!

WILDWOOD FLOWER

Traditional, Late 1800s

EIGHTH NOTES

We're about to encounter some tunes with **eighth notes**. Two eighth notes equal one quarter note in value.

1 quarter note ♩ = 2 eighth notes ♫

One eighth note is written with a flag (♪). Consecutive eighth notes are connected with a beam (♫).

To count eighth notes, say "and" in between the beats. In 4/4 time, there are eight eighth notes in a measure.

Try these eighth notes. Go slowly and evenly, and count "1 and 2 and 3 and 4 and."

The next tune mixes quarter and eighth notes.

FRÉRE JACQUES
(Are You Sleeping?)

Children's Melody

First, play this melody using mostly quarter notes.

SHORTENING BREAD

Southern Folk Song

Mama's little baby loves short-nin', short-nin', mama's little baby loves short-nin' bread.

Now, play the same melody using eighth notes. As always, play very slowly at first, then gradually work up to speed.

SHORTENING BREAD
Puttin' It All Together

Ma - ma's lit - tle ba - by loves short - nin', short - nin',

Ma - ma's lit - tle ba - by loves short - nin' bread. Ma - ma's lit - tle ba - by loves

short - nin', short - nin', Ma - ma's lit - tle ba - by loves short - nin' bread.

"The ukulele became the official instrument of the Islands when King Kalakaua took it up in 1886 and featured it for the first time with hula dancers."

—Acoustic Guitar and Other Fretted Instruments

LITTLE BROWN JUG

Minstrel
Old Time Country

"The ukulele had this advantage: not even a trained musician could tell if you were really playing it or just monkeying around with it." —*Will Rogers*

PLAYING CHORDS

C Chord

F Chord

G7 Chord

A **chord** is a combination of three or more notes played together. The chord frames above are like maps of your ukulele's fret-board. As you've seen with single notes, the dots show which strings to depress at which frets. The numbers on the dots tell you which fingers to use. To play a C chord, for example, use the tip of the second finger of your left hand and depress the A string just behind the third fret. Strum all four strings with your right hand, and voilà! Now try the F and G7 chords.

Practice these chords by brushing down with your thumb across all four strings. Strum once for each slash in the measure. Note: concentrate on using your fingertips to depress the strings where shown, so that your fingers don't touch any of the wrong strings.

STRUMMING CHORDS

Once you've learned some basic chords, it's time to begin working on some simple strumming techniques. The most basic way to strum chords is with your thumb, as shown.

THUMB BRUSH STRUM

With your hand relaxed, let your thumb gently brush across the strings in a downward pattern.

COUNT: 1 – 2 – 3 – 4

Each time you brush down across all four strings, lift your hand back up without touching the strings and bring your hand back down to brush again. Do this until you can get a smooth rhythmic beat.

Using this familiar two-chord melody, practice the thumb brush strum while singing the words to "Hush Little Baby."

Hush little baby, don't say a word, Mama's gonna buy you a mockingbird.

And if that mockingbird don't sing, Mama's gonna buy you a diamond ring.

FIRST-FINGER STRUM

The thumb brush may be the most basic way to strum, but the first-finger strum is the most common way to strum your ukulele. Make a loose fist with your right hand and let your first (pointer) finger curl out as shown. Place your hand over the lower fretboard and using the tip of your finger, strum down.

As you did with the thumb, brush down across all four strings, lift your hand back up without touching the strings, then brush down again.

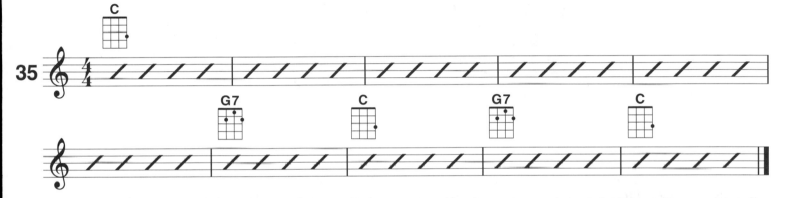

12-BAR BLUES

The basic blues progression below is called a **12-bar blues**, because it has twelve measures. From rock to country to pop, the 12-bar blues is the foundation upon which much of American music rests. It is the heartbeat of Chuck Berry, Bill Haley, Jerry Lee Lewis, and hundreds of others.

Practice this chord progression strumming slowly with this rhythmic strum pattern: down, down–up, down–up, down–up.
(Count: 1 2 & 3 & 4 &)

GENERIC BLUES

FINGER AND THUMB STRUM

Now that you are comfortable strumming with your thumb and your first finger, let's combine them to create an interesting rhythm. The time signature is 4/4, four beats per measure. The count is "1–2–3–and–4."

1. Brush down with your finger on beat 1.

2. Brush down with your finger again on beat 2.

3. Brush down again with your finger following quickly with your thumb, on beat 3.

4. Following quickly, brush up with your finger on the "and" of beat 3 (the eighth note after beat 3).

5. Brush down with your finger again on beat 4.

There are many variations that you can play. Below is a graphic example of the main strum pattern and a slight variation of it. The arrows represent downstrokes and upstrokes; F = finger, T = thumb.

Practice this very slowly until you can keep a steady rhythmic beat of "1–2–a–3–and–4." It helps to count out loud.

STRUM IT

26

THE G CHORD FAMILY
G, C, D7, and Em Chords

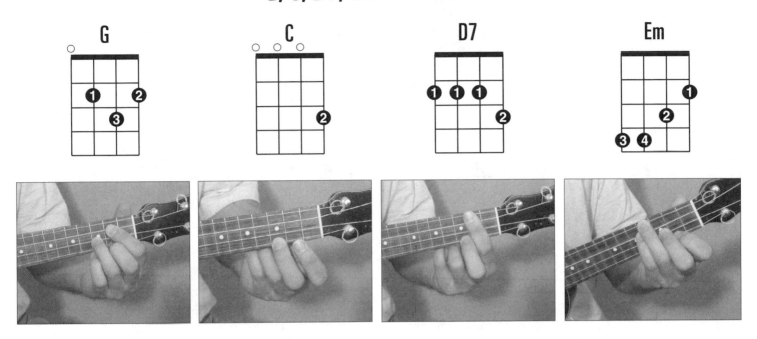

Repeat this progression until you can change chords smoothly. Try playing it with the finger strum pattern in the following exercise.

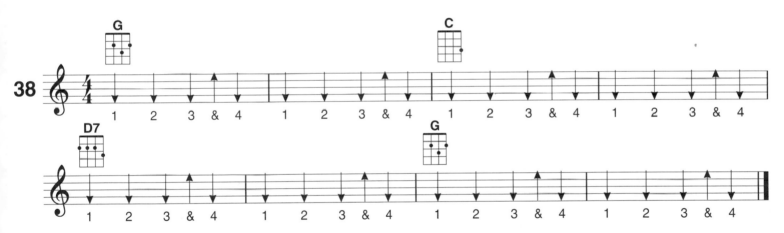

Now try the "Ooh-Wah Uke" progression in the key of G. Use the finger and thumb strum and variation that you just learned.

OOH-WAH UKE

First, become comfortable with picking out this melody. Then go back and learn the rhythm part by strumming the chords.

BOIL 'EM CABBAGE DOWN

Bluegrass

3/4 TIME

While most of the songs we have studied so far have had four beats per measure, **3/4 time** has only three beats per measure. One of the most common 3/4 patterns is called **waltz time**. A waltz is an old-fashioned dance that originated in Eastern Europe around the beginning of the eighteenth century. Today, this rhythm is an important part of American music.

THREE BEATS PER MEASURE
QUARTER NOTE (♩) = ONE BEAT

COUNT: 1   2   3

We count: ONE–two–three,
             ONE–two–three,
             ONE–two–three.

Or we count: OOM–pah–pah,
                OOM–pah–pah,
                OOM–pah–pah.

There are literally thousands of songs in 3/4 or waltz time, including "Goodnight Irene," "Tennessee Waltz," "Melody of Love," "After the Ball," "Scarborough Fair," "Streets of Laredo," and "Norwegian Wood."

Here's a 3/4 picking exercise using the G and B notes. Count as you pick.

WALTZ

Hawaii's late Queen Liliuakalami once said that the word ukulele meant "the gift that came home." *Uku* means "gift," and *lele* translates as "to come."

—*Old Time Herald*

Try this exercise in 3/4 time using the thumb brush strum.

PLAYING THE 3/4 STRUM

Here's one of the many ways to strum in 3/4 time:

1. Position your pointer finger over the fretboard as if you're about to strum;
2. finger a G chord;
3. strum down on beat 1, putting emphasis on that beat;
4. strum down again on beat 2;
5. follow that quickly with an up-strum on the "and" of beat 2;
6. finish with one final strum on beat 3.

The whole thing looks like this:

Now let's give it a try.

WALTZ STRUM

Play this well-known melody, then play the chord part using the 3/4 strum.

AMAZING GRACE

By John Newton

Arrangment by
Lil' Rev and John Nicolson

John Newton was the captain of a slave ship. While sailing on the high seas, he experienced a religious conversion and returned to Africa to set his captives free. He went on to pen many classic hymns, but this one took on a life of its own.

THE F CHORD FAMILY
F, B♭, and C7 Chords

F

B♭

C7

Try playing the F chord all by itself.

45 F

Now let's add the C7 chord.

46 F — C7 — F

Hush lit-tle ba - by   don't say a word.   Ma-ma's gon-na buy you a   mock - ing - bird.

C7 — F

If   that mock - ing - bird don't sing,   Ma-ma's gon-na buy you a   dia - mond ring.

Finally, let's add the B♭ chord.

47 F — B♭

F — C7 — F

32

Try strumming the following exercise à la "Rolling in My Sweet Baby's Arms." The finger strum pattern is easy to hear and follow. Your goal is to change chords smoothly without breaking the flow. When you can do this, you'll be ready to learn other songs in the key of F.

ROLLING

JUKING THE UKE

While the most common type of blues structure is the 12-bar (because it has twelve measures), blues tunes come in all shapes and sizes, from eight, twelve, sixteen, to even thirty-two bars. Here's an eight-bar example. The finger strum pattern is easy to hear and follow.

Lil' Rev

SHARPS AND FLATS

The symbol ♯ stands for **sharp** and raises the pitch by a half step (or one fret). When you see the sharp symbol before a note on the staff line, you raise that note by playing up one fret. Conversely, when you see the **flat** symbol (♭), you play that note one fret down.

F-SHARP (F♯)

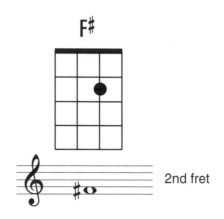

2nd fret

DOWN IN THE VALLEY

Southern Folk Song

Down in the val - ley, val - ley so low._____ Hang your head o - ver, hear the wind blow._____

Now try playing the chords to this tune.

KEY SIGNATURES

One convenient way to avoid assigning a flat (♭) to every B in a piece of music is to simply put a flat sign at the beginning of each line. Then every time you see a B note, you play a B♭. This is called a **key signature** and it works for all kinds of sharps and flats. The exercises below use the key signature.

B-FLAT (B♭)

1st fret

PRACTICE TIP

Regular practice is essential. Practicing a half hour each day is better than practicing two hours every four days. Find a regular time of the day that works for you.

THE F MAJOR SCALE

Now that you know the B♭ note, you know all the notes in the F major scale. The key signature (with B flatted) tells us that we're in the key of F. Notice the new note high F. Play this with your pinky finger on the 8th fret of the first string.

CLEMENTINE

Moving up the F major scale:

Now let's try playing a basic melody in the key of F using our thumb to pick each note. Go slowly first and gradually pick up speed.

PAW PAW PATCH

Traditional Folk

Where, oh, where is dear lit-tle Nel-lie? Where, oh, where is dear lit-tle Nel-lie?

Where, oh, where is dear lit-tle Nel-lie? Way down yon-der in the paw paw patch.

Here's a great melody for you to practice in the key of F. After you can pick the melody well, go back and try to sing and strum while tapping out the rhythm with your foot.

SKIP TO MY LOU

American Game Song

Skip, skip, skip to my Lou, skip, skip, skip to my Lou,

skip, skip, skip to my Lou, skip to my Lou my dar - ling.

Notice the new key signature in these next two songs. Remember to play every F note one half step higher to F♯.

IN THE MOON'S PALE SHIMMER
(Au Claire de la Lune)

French Folk Song

Watch for F♯s in the thirteenth and fifteenth measures.

SHE'LL BE COMING 'ROUND THE MOUNTAIN

Folk Song

THE SINGLE ROLL STROKE

The roll stroke is a lively rhythmic strumming technique that emphasizes the downbeat of the strum by unraveling your right-hand fingers one-by-one. When properly executed, it should sound like one continuous flowing beat.

Think of flicking a tiny ball of paper off a desk with one finger. Then, imagine flicking four tiny balls of paper (one after the other) with one continuous motion of your four fingers. This is in effect what you are doing with a roll stroke.

1. Bring your right-hand pinky down across all four strings.

2. Let your third (ring) finger follow right after your pinky.

3. Now your second (middle) finger follows down across all four strings.

4. Finally, bring your pointer finger down across all of the strings.

Think of your fingers unraveling in a steady progression, one after the next. When this is mastered, you can try adding your thumb, which will follow right after the pointer finger in its downward motion.

At the end of "Shave and a Haircut," try the roll stroke on the D7 chord, then quickly over the G chord. This may take a little practice, but it's well worth the effort. When notes and tablature are shown in stacks as seen below, this indicates a chord, or a group of notes played simultaneously.

SHAVE AND A HAIRCUT

Bluegrass Lick

This lick is traditionally used to end songs. When you have it up to speed, you can use it to end songs in the key of G (including "Boil 'Em Cabbage Down").

Beverly Uke-a-Billy Challenge: See if you can figure out how to play this lick in other keys.

PLAYING TREMOLO

Tremolo is a very beautiful and pleasing sound when played on the ukulele. Here's how to do it:

1. Spread the fingers of your right hand as shown.

2. Position your pointer over the tenth fret.

3. Using the pad of your fingertip, gently yet rapidly rub all four strings in a continuous and even up-and-down motion.

The musical symbol we will use for tremolo is (𝄎).

Go back to page 18 and review the melody for "Aura Lee." Once you have it in your head, play this chord progression using tremolo. Notice the new E7 chord. This is just like the D7 chord fingering that you know, but up two frets. There is also another new chord here that is easy to play: Am. Look at the next page for the Am chord fingering. Count "1–2–3–4" for each measure.

AURA LEE

Blowin' In The Wind
Bob Dylan

```
G          C          G
How many roads must a man walk down
         C          D
Before you call him a man?
       G          C          G
Yes, 'n' how many seas must a white
dove sail
           C              D
Before she sleeps in the sand?
       G          C          G
Yes, 'n' how many times must the cannon
balls fly
           C          D
Before they're for-ever banned?

      C           D      G
The answer, my friend, is blowin' in the
  Em
wind,
         C         D          G
The answer is blowin' in the wind.


G          C              G
How many years can a mountain exist
       C              D
Before it's washed to the sea?
       G          C          G
Yes, 'n' how many years can some people
exist
             C          D
Before they're allowed to be free?
         G          C          G
Yes, 'n' how many times can a man turn
his head,
             C              D
And pretend that he just doesn't see?
```

```
      C          D      G
The answer, my friend, is blowin' in the
 Em
wind,
         C         D          G
The answer is blowin' in the wind.


G          C              G
How many times must a man look up
             C      D
Before he can see the sky?
       G          C          G
Yes, 'n' how many ears must one man
have
                 C          D
Before he can hear people cry?
         G          C          G
Yes, 'n' how many deaths will it take till
he knows
                 C          D
That too many people have died?

      C          D      G
The answer, my friend, is blowin' in the
 Em
wind,
         C         D          G
The answer is blowin' in the wind.

      C          D      G
The answer, my friend, is blowin' in the
 Em
wind,
         C         D          G
The answer is blowin' in the wind.
```

This Land is your Land Words & Music by Woody Guthrie

Intro: C chord

C   F   G7   Am   C7

CHORUS
```
        F                         C
This land is your land this land is my land
    G7                        C    C7
From California to the New York island
                        F              C    Am
From the red wood forest to the Gulf Stream waters
 G7                       C    C7
This land was made for you and me


           F                   C
As I was walking that ribbon of highway
        G7              C    C7
I saw above me that endless skyway
           F                C    Am
I saw below me that golden valley
 G7                     C    C7
This land was made for you and me


              F                        C
I've roamed & rambled and I followed my footsteps
                G7              C    C7
To the sparkling sands of her diamond deserts
              F              C    Am
And all around me a voice was sounding
 G7                     C    C7
This land was made for you and me


              F                 C
When the sun came shining, and I was strolling
                   G7                      C    C7
& the wheat fields waving & the dust clouds rolling
              F              C    Am
As the fog was lifting a voice was chanting
 G7                     C    C7
This land was made for you and me


          F              C
As I went walking I saw a sign there
            G7              C    C7
And on the sign it said "No Trespassing"
            F                  C    Am
But on the other side it didn't say nothing
 G7                     C    C7
That side was made for you and me


              F                         C
In the squares of the city, in the shadow of a steeple
            G7              C    C7
By the relief office I seen my people
                         F              C    Am
As they stood there hungry, I stood there asking
  G7                    C    C7
Is this land made for you and me?


          F              C
Nobody living can ever stop me
            G7              C    C7
As I go walking that freedom highway
            F              C    Am
Nobody living can ever make me turn back
 G7                     C    C7
This land was made for you and me
```

Annie's Song - John Denver *

Intro in ¾: [C] [Csus4] [C] [Csus4] [C]

You [Csus4] fill up my [F] sen[G]ses [Am],
Like a [F] night in the [C] forest [Em] [Am]
Like the [G] mountains in [F] spring [Em] time [Dm],
Like a [F] walk in the [G] rain [Gsus4] [G]
Like a [Gsus4] storm [G] in the [F] des[G]ert [Am],
Like a [F] sleepy blue [C] ocean [Em] [Am]
You [G] fill up my [F] sen[Em]ses [Dm],
Come [G] fill me a[C]gain [Csus4] [C]

[Csus4] Come let me [F] love [G] you [Am],
Let me [F] give my life [C] to you [Em] [Am]
Let me [G] drown in your [F] laugh[Em]ter [Dm]
Let me [F] die in your [G] arms [Gsus4] [G]
Let me [Gsus4] lay [G] down be[F]side [G] you [Am]
Let me al[F]ways be [C] with you [Em] [Am]
Come [G] let me [F] love [Em] you [Dm]
Come [G] love me a[C]gain [Csus4] [C]

Interlude
[Csus4] [F] [G] [Am]
[F]   [C]   [Em]   [Am]
[G]   [F]   [Em]   [Dm]
[F]   [G]   [Gsus4]   [G]
[Gsus4] [G] [F] [G]   [Am]

Let me [F] give my life [C] to you [Em] [Am]
Come [G] let me [F] love [Em] you [Dm]
Come [G7] love me a[C]gain [Csus4] [C]

You [Csus4] fill up my [F] sen[G]ses [Am],
Like a [F] night in the [C] forest [Em] [Am]
Like the [G] mountains in [F] spring[Em]time [Dm]
Like a [F] walk in the [G] rain [Gsus4] [G]
Like a [Gsus4] storm [G] in the [F] des[G]ert [Am],
Like a [F] sleepy blue [C] ocean [Em] [Am]
You [G] fill up my [F] sen[Em]ses [Dm]
Come [G] fill me a[C]gain [Csus4] [C] [Csus4] [C]

*John Denver sings in the key of D major (capo on 2)

http://www.anneku.com

OVER THE RAINBOW / WONDERFUL WORLD
by Israël Kamakawiwo'ole

Intro:

```
|C    G    |Am   F   |C    G    |
|Am        |F        |          |

    C          Em         F          C
  ooo-ooo    ooo-ooo    ooo-ooo    ooo-ooo
    F          E7         Am         F
  ooo-ooo    ooo-ooo    ooo-ooo    ooo-ooo
```

```
C              Em                  F          C
Somewhere over the rainbow, way up high
F there's a land that I heard of               G            Am    F
And the dreams that you dream of once in a lullaby...
     C              Em              F          C
Oh somewhere over the rainbow, blue birds fly
F         C              dare to    G              Am    F
And the dreams that you dream of, dreams really do come true...


         C
Someday i'll wish upon a star
G                                        Am    F
Wake up where the clouds are far behind me
          C
Where trouble melts like lemon drops
G                                    Am          F
High above the chimney tops that's where you'll find me


       C          Em              F          C
Oh somewhere over the rainbow, blue birds fly
F         C                      G              Am    F
```

```
      F          G                              G            Am  F
And the dreams that you dare to, oh why, oh why can't I?...


            C        Em          F        C
Well I see trees of green and Red roses too
F                 C            E7      Am
  I'll watch then bloom for me and you
        F                  G              Am    F
And I think to myself: what a wonderful world
            C        Em          F        C
Well I see skies of blue and I see clouds of white
        F      of the  C   E7       E7   Am          Am
And the brightness of day, I like the dark of the night
        F                  G           C   F   C
And I think to myself: what a wonderful world


     G                      C
The colours of the rainbow so pretty in the sky
     G                      C
Are also on the faces of people passing bye
     F              C      F            C
I See friends shaking hands, saying 'how do you do?'
F              C        Dm7          D
  They're really saying, I...I love you


          C        Em          F        C
I hear babies cry and I watch them grow
F    re gonna        C    E7    I       Am
  They'll learn much more than we'll know
                                    ever
      F                  G              Am    F
And I think to myself: what a wonderful world


C
Someday i'll wish upon a star
G                                Am    F
and Wake up where the clouds are far behind me
            C
Where trouble melts like lemon drops
G                                Am         F
a way High above the chimney tops that's where you'll find me


     C        Em          F    C
Oh somewhere over the rainbow, way up high
F        C                    G            Am    F
And the dreams that you dare to, why, oh why can't I?...
                    dream


C        Em          F        C
ooo-ooo  ooo-ooo  ooo-ooo  ooo-ooo
```

```
F           E7          Am          F
ooo-ooo     ooo-ooo     ooo-a-eh-a-a-a-a-a-a
```

This arrangement for the song is the author's own work and represents their interpretation of the song. You may only use this for private study, scholarship, or research. UkuWorld and its derivatives do not own any songs, lyrics or arrangements posted and/or printed.

WHAT A WONDERFUL WORLD
by Louis Armstrong

Verse:
```
        F         C       Dm          Am
I see trees of green, red roses too
Gm          F        A7          Dm
I see them bloom, for me and you,
        Bb             C              F
And I think to myself, What a wonderful world.
```

Verse:
```
        F         C       Dm          Am
I see skies of blue and clouds of white,
Gm                   F        A7          Dm
The bright blessed day, the dark sacred night,
        Bb             C              F
And I think to myself, what a wonderful world
```

Verse:
```
       C                          F
The colours of a rainbow are so pretty in the sky
C                        F
Are also on the faces of people going by
          Dm          Am          Dm          Am
I see friends shaking hands saying how do you do
Dm          Am      F       C
They're really saying I love you.
```

Verse:
```
        F       C     Dm          Am
I hear babies cry, I watch them grow
Gm              F    A7            Dm
They'll learn much more than I'll ever know,
        Bb             C              F
And I think to myself what a wonderful world
```

```
      Bb                  C                 F
Yes I think to myself, what a wonderful world.
```

CITY OF NEW ORLEANS - by Steve Goodman

[G] Ridin' on the [D] City of New [G] Orleans,
[Em] Illinois Central, [C] Monday morning [G]rail
Fifteen cars and [D] fifteen restless [G] riders,
Three [Em] conductors, and [D] 25 sacks of [G] mail
All a- [Em] long the southbound Odyssey
The [Bm] train pulls out of Kankakee
And [D] rolls along the houses, farms and [A] fields
[Em] Passin' towns that have no name,
And [Bm] freight-yards full of old black men
And the [D] graveyards of the [D7] rusted automo-[G]biles [G7]

===== CHORUS:
[C] Good morning [D7] America how [G] are you? {Last Chorus "Good NIGHT"}
Say, [Em] don't you know me [C] I'm your native [G] son
[D7] I'm the [G] train they call the [D] City of New [Em] Orleans
I'll be [F] gone five [C] hundred [D] miles when the day is [G] done
=================

[G]Dealin' card games with the [D] old men in the [G] club car
[Em] Penny a point ain't [C] no one keeping [G] score
Pass the paper [D] bag that holds the [G] bottle
[Em] Feel the wheels [D] grumblin' 'neath the [G] floor
[Em] And the sons of Pullman porters and the [Bm] sons of engineers
Ride their [D] father's magic carpet made of [A] steel
[Em] Mothers with their babes asleep are [Bm] rockin' to the gentle beat
And the [D] rhythm of the [D7] rails is all they [G] feel [G7}

CHORUS

[G] Nighttime on the [D] City of [G] New Orleans
[Em] Changin' cars in [C] Memphis, [G] Tennesee
Halfway home, [D] we'll be there by [G] mornin'
[Em] Through the Mississippi darkness [D] rollin' down to the [G] sea
[Em] But all the towns and people seem to [Bm] fade into a bad dream
And the [D] steel rail still ain't heard the [A] news
[Em] The conductor sings his songs again
[Bm] the passengers will please refrain
[D] This train's got the [D7] disappearin' railroad [G] blues [G7]

CHORUS

The Am Chord

Am

Familiarize yourself with this new chord, and get re-acquainted with the C, F, and G7 chord shapes. Then try playing "Doo-Wop Uke" using tremolo. Work toward keeping the tremolo going smoothly by switching from chord to chord without losing the beat. Remember to use the pad of your pointer finger.

DOO-WOP UKE

RESTS

Music is made up of both sound and silence. Silence is represented by musical symbols called **rests**. They are just as important as the notes you play. Each type of note has a corresponding rest of the same name and duration:

Remember to count while you do these exercises.

Sometimes it helps to tap your foot during rests to keep time.

"Goodnight Ladies" contains both quarter rests and eighth rests. Notice the key signature!

GOODNIGHT LADIES

| Good | - | night | | la | - | dies, | | good | - | night | | la | - | dies, |
| good | - | night | | la | - | dies | we're | | going | to | leave | you | | now. |

MERRILY WE ROLL ALONG

| Mer | - | ri | - | ly | we | roll | a | - | long, | | roll | a | - | long, | | roll | a | - | long, |
| mer | - | ri | - | ly | we | roll | a | - | long, | | o | - | ver | the | deep | blue | | sea. |

THE E MINOR CHORD FAMILY
Em, Am, and B7 Chords

You already used the Am in "Doo Wop Uke"; now meet its relatives in the E minor family.

Minor chords offer a nice contrast to the bright sounds of the major and seventh chords we have seen. Some folks describe the sound of minor chords as "spooky" or "sad."

Let's start by strumming the Em chord.

Em

67

Now mix it up with the Am chord.

Em **Am** **Em** **Am** **Em**

68

Try this 8-bar minor blues progression.

Em **B7** **Am**

69

1 2 3 & 4 &   1 2 3 & 4 &   1 2 3 & 4 &   1 2 3 & 4 &

Em **B7** **Em** **B7**

1 2 3 & 4 &   1 2 3 & 4 &   1 2 3 & 4 &   1 2 3 & 4 &

Here's a typical 12-bar minor blues progression in Em. Remember to count "1–2–3–4." Try mixing it up as you play this tune and use several different strum patterns that you've learned.

THE HAUNTED UKE BLUES

Blues Progression

70 My house is getting haunted, there must be spooks all in my uke.

My house is getting haunted, there must be spooks all in my

uke. Everytime I play a tune,

it just comes out oh so blue.

Try picking out this minor melody using your thumb.

HEY, HO, NOBODY HOME

English Folk Melody

71 Hey, ho, no - bod - y home, meat nor drink nor

mon - ey have I none yet will I be mer - ry.

MORE CHORDS

Get familiar with the chord positions shown, then practice changing between the chords.

72

Now let's really mix it up!

73

Here's a challenge: try changing chords every one or two beats instead of every four. Practice slowly at first and gradually work up to speed.

74

Now that you're familiar with the Dm chord, let's play a minor melody. Go slowly and pay attention to each note's time value. Gradually work up to playing a little faster. There's a new chord in "Scarborough Fair" that you haven't seen yet, the A chord. You can find this chord and many others in the Chord Chart at the back of the book.

SINNER MAN

SCARBOROUGH FAIR

CHORD CHART

Here are all the chords we used in this book, and some other common chords you may encounter in your ukulele adventures.

MAJOR	**MINOR**	**7TH**
C	Cm	C7
D	Dm	D7
E	Em	E7
F	Fm	F7
G	Gm	G7
A	Am	A7
B♭	B♭m	B♭7
B	Bm	B7

48